Helping Children See Jesus

ISBN: 978-1-64104-070-9

Judgment
The Wrath of God
*New Testament Volume 44:
Revelation Part 3*

Author: Ruth B. Greiner
Illustrator: Vernon Henkel
Computer Graphic Artist: Ed Olson
Typesetting and Layout: Patricia Pope

© 2018 Bible Visuals International
PO Box 153, Akron, PA 17501-0153
Phone: (717) 859-1131
www.biblevisuals.org

All rights reserved. No part of this publication may be reproduced, stored in a retrieval system or transmitted in any form by any means, electronic, mechanical, photocopy, recording or otherwise, without the prior permission of the publisher, except as provided by USA copyright law.

RELATED ITEMS

To access related items (such as activities, memory verse posters and translated texts) please visit our web store at www.biblevisuals.org and enter 1044 at the top right of the web page. You may need to reduce the zoom setting to get the search box.

FREE TEXT DOWNLOAD

To obtain a FREE printable copy of the English teaching text (PDF format) under Product Format, please scroll down and select Extra–PDF Teacher Text Download. Then under Language select English before clicking the ADD TO CART button to place in your shopping cart. Other languages are available at an additional cost from the Language menu. When checking out, use coupon code XTACSV17 at checkout and click on Apply Coupon to receive the discount on the English text.

Shall not the Judge of all the earth do right?

Genesis 18:25b

Lesson 1
THE SEVEN SEALS

NOTE TO THE TEACHER

From the Gospel accounts, we learn about the Lord Jesus as He was on earth–a Saviour, dying for sinners. Revelation shows Him as He is now and will be–a Priest-King, judging sin. Everything in this book centers around Him, for this is the *Revelation of Jesus Christ.*

Beginning in Revelation 4 the events move along as they may in a story book or play. That is, we go to a certain point and stop there. Then we look at some other events and learn of other characters and what was happening to them in the meantime. Some of the events take place in Heaven; others, on earth; then back to Heaven again. Hints are given of things which are going to occur later.

It is good to keep the outline of the book in mind:

1. "The things which thou hast seen" (Revelation 1:1-20). (John's vision of the Lord Jesus Christ)
2. "The things which are" (Revelation 2:1–3:22). (The spiritual condition of the churches of John's day–and typical of churches today.)
3. "The things which shall be after these things" (Revelation 4:1–22:21). (These are the things which will take place *after* the Church is taken up out of the world. See 1 Thessalonians 4:13-18.)

It is the understanding of the publishers of this series that the rapture (or *the translation of the believers*) occurs *before* the events which are recorded in chapters 4 through 22. This means that all who have trusted in Christ the Lord will meet Him in the air and go with Him to Heaven. There they will be safe with Him during the years of awful tribulation on Earth.

Your students need a clear understanding of God's plan for the future. Before starting this volume, why not review New Testament Volume 32 entitled *The Future of the Church*. The end of the first lesson and all of the second will be helpful.

Have your class list in their notebooks the symbols (and their meanings!) which appear in this lesson. (Refer to the chart on page 9.) Keeping their Bibles and notebooks open, they should be urged to tell what each symbol means as the lesson progresses. On Illustration #1, print as follows:

Seal #1   FALSE PEACE
Seal #2   WAR
Seal #3   FAMINE
Seal #4   DEATH

There is no illustration for Seal #5.

Suggestion: Because of the many details of this volume, you may want to divide each lesson into one or two sessions.

Scripture to be studied: Revelation 6:1–8:6

The *aim* of the lesson: To show that although God is love, He will punish severely.

What your students should *know:* God has the right to judge the earth–and He will!

What your students should *feel:* Terrified for those who will endure the tribulation.

What your students should *do:* Be faithful witnesses so others may escape the judgment to come.

Lesson outline (for the teacher's and students' notebooks):

1. The first four seals opened: (1) A lie promising peace; (2) War; (3) Famine; (4) Death (Revelation 6:1-8).
2. The fifth and sixth seals opened: (5) Martyred believers calling for judgment; (6) The heavens and earth disturbed (Revelation 6:9-17).
3. God's protection for those saved in the tribulation (Revelation 7:1-17).
4. The seventh seal opened: Seven angels receive trumpets (Revelation 8:1-6).

The verse to be memorized:

Shall not the Judge of all the earth do right?
(Genesis 18:25b)

THE LESSON

If we read the last chapter of a book without having read any of the other chapters, we usually become confused. We have to know what happens before the end of the book if we are going to understand the last chapter perfectly. So it is with the book of Revelation–the last part of the Bible. We should know what is taught in all the other books. For example, what Isaiah, Ezekiel, Daniel and the other Old Testament prophets wrote helps us to understand the book of Revelation. Remember that even before time began on earth, God had a plan for everything.

Show Illustration #1

(*Teacher:* Point to arrow on left.) He knew exactly when His Son would come to earth. He knew that everybody would need a perfect sacrifice for their sins. And Christ the Saviour would be that sacrifice. (*Teacher:* Print on first arrow: *Christ Comes as Saviour.*) God planned that after the Lord Jesus died and rose again, He would return to His home in Heaven. (*Teacher:* Point to second arrow and print on it: *Christ Ascends to Heaven.*) For almost 2,000 years, God the Son has been sitting next to God the Father.

There is still more in the program which God has planned. Someday, though we are not told when, the Lord Jesus will come in the clouds and catch up all who have trusted in Him. (*Teacher:* Point to third arrow and print: *Rapture–Translation of Believers.*) All the believers who are living at the time of His coming, plus the believers who have died, will be taken up to meet the Lord in the air. And they will be with Him forever. (See 1 Corinthians 15:51-52; 1 Thessalonians 4:13-18.)

It is our understanding that after the believers are taken up into Heaven, there will be dreadful suffering on earth. This time of suffering is often spoken of as *The Tribulation*. (*Teacher:* Print *Tribulation* between the third and fourth arrows.) After the tribulation the Lord Christ will come again to earth. (*Teacher:* Point to fourth arrow and print: *Christ Comes to Reign.*) This time He will come as King to reign on earth for 1,000 years. When He comes, He will bring with Him the believers He had taken up with Him. And they will reign with Him. Will you go up with Him (*Teacher:* Point to third arrow.) and come again with Him? (*Teacher:* Point to fourth arrow. Encourage student discussion. Make it perfectly clear that only those who have truly placed their trust in Christ will be with Him.)

In our last lesson we learned that the Lamb (Jesus Christ) was the only one in Heaven found worthy to open the scroll which came from God. On the scroll were seven seals to be opened. Today we shall see that the seals were opened one at a time. John saw up there in Heaven hundreds of years ago, things which are going to happen someday in the future. We don't know the dates of these events. But we understand they will take place while all believers are up in Heaven with the Lord. Do you want to know about the tribulation on earth? Listen carefully!

1. THE FIRST FOUR SEALS OPENED
Revelation 6:1-8

Christ broke open the first of the seven seals. A voice thundered, "Come!"

Show Illustration #2A

A beautiful white horse appeared. The rider on the horse had a bow, but no arrows. A crown was given him, and he rode out to win.

This means that in the beginning of the tribulation a man will appear promising to bring peace to the earth. (The bow without arrows seems to promise peace.) He will come imitating Christ. But really he will be against Christ–the anti-Christ. The Bible speaks of him as the *Man of Sin*, the lawless one, a great deceiver. (See 2 Thessalonians 2:3-12; Matthew 24:5.) Can you guess to whose kingdom this man belongs? *(Satan's)*

Show Illustration #2B

The Lord Jesus broke open the second seal. Out came a fiery red horse. The rider was handed a mighty sword. He was given power to make war.

The sword and the red horse tell us that there will be bloody warfare on earth during the tribulation. (See Ezekiel 38:21; Matthew 24:6-7.)

Show Illustration #2C

When the Lamb of God broke the third seal, a black horse came out. The rider carried scales for weighing food.

God is warning that during the tribulation there won't be enough food. (See Matthew 24:7.) And for the food that there is, people will have to pay eight times the usual cost. So, many will starve to death when the tribulation comes to earth.

Show Illustration #2D

When Christ broke the fourth seal, out came a yellowish green, pale horse. Its rider was named "Death." These were given the right to kill one-fourth of the people.

So God is giving notice that one-fourth of the population on Earth will die at this time in the tribulation. Oh, what suffering there will be in those days! (See Matthew 24:4, 6-7.)

2. THE FIFTH AND SIXTH SEALS OPENED
Revelation 6:9-17

Then the Lord broke open the fifth seal of the scroll. John saw those who had been killed for telling others that they had trusted in Christ. They begged God to punish those who had murdered them. (*Teacher:* The fact that these souls were "under the altar" in Heaven is a reminder of the Old Testament sacrifices. The blood of those sacrifices was poured out at the bottom of the altar. See Leviticus 4:25.)

God wants us to know that during the tribulation on earth, some will place their trust in Christ. But they will pay with their lives. They will want the Lord to punish their murderers. But God will tell them that they must wait until others are also martyred. Then their prayers will be answered.

Show Illustration #3

The Lord then opened the sixth seal. Now watch what will happen next during the tribulation on Earth.

There will be a great earthquake. The sun will be darkened. The moon will be reddened. Stars will fall to earth. The heavens will open for a moment so people on earth can see God on His throne. Every mountain and island will be moved.

People will be terrified. They will pray to the mountains and rocks, "Fall on us! Hide us from the face of Him who sits on the throne! Save us from the wrath of the Lamb!" (See Luke 21:25-26; 23:30.)

Wars, famine, death, earthquakes–none of these will affect those who are against the Lord during the tribulation. But when they get one glimpse of God on His throne, they will try to hide from Him. (See Isaiah 2:19.)

3. GOD'S PROTECTION FOR THOSE SAVED IN THE TRIBULATION
Revelation 7:1-17

Although God is a righteous Judge, He is also merciful. Before the seventh seal was opened, John saw four angels holding back the winds of the earth. A fifth angel appeared carrying the seal (or mark) of the living God. He commanded the other angels, "Do not harm the earth or the sea or the trees. Hold off the judgment until we have put the seal on the foreheads of the servants of our God."

Show Illustration #4

Who are these who will receive God's mark of ownership during the dreadful days of tribulation? They are 144,000 Jewish people: 12,000 from each of the 12 tribes. They will confess that Jesus Christ is the Lord. They will be owned and protected by the living God of Heaven.

There will be others who will be saved during the tribulation on earth. John saw a great multitude before God's throne–more than can be numbered. They will come from Africa, Europe, Asia, America, Australia, the islands of the sea. (See Matthew 25:31-40.) Wearing white robes, they will wave palms of victory. Who are they? "These are the ones who have come out of the great tribulation, the time of great trouble. They have washed their robes and made them white in the blood of the Lamb . . . They serve God day and night in His temple . . . the Lamb in the midst of the throne is their Shepherd . . . and God shall wipe every tear from their eyes."

How will this group from all over the world hear the Gospel during the tribulation? Doubtless from the 144,000 saved Jews.

We cannot know how dreadful the tribulation years will be. All those who are born-again believers before the tribulation starts will be up in Heaven. But God will always save those who place their trust in His Son. Apparently all who turn to Him during the tribulation are people who never before had heard the Gospel. Those who deliberately reject or ignore the Lord before the tribulation, will have no second chance. God will cause them to believe the devil's lies during the tribulation, for they would not receive Christ when they could have. (See 2 Thessalonians 2:8-12.)

4. THE SEVENTH SEAL OPENED
Revelation 8:1-6

John had already seen much that is going to happen in the future. Yet there was another seal to be opened. The Lamb of God broke the seventh seal. John held his breath. But there was no sound in Heaven for about half an hour.

Show Illustration #5

John saw seven angels standing before God. To each was given a trumpet. What will happen when the trumpets are sounded? We shall have to wait until our next lesson. Then we shall learn more about the future.

War, famine, many deaths, earthquakes, the upheaval in the skies, people martyred for believing in Christ–all of this suffering and much, much more will occur during the awful time of tribulation. But you won't have to go through it–not if you have placed your trust in the Lord Jesus, the Lamb of God. If you have never received Him, will you do so right now?

If you are already a child of God, are you concerned for others who don't know Him? Have you done all you can to lead them to the Saviour? Will you write in your notebook the names of those whom you would like to introduce to Christ this week? Then we will ask the Lord to give you that opportunity.

Lesson 2
THE SEVEN TRUMPETS

NOTE TO THE TEACHER

Give serious thought to this lesson as you pray and prepare to teach it. God doesn't want one soul to perish eternally . (See 2 Peter 3:9.) Nor does He want anyone to go through the tribulation. The warnings of judgment which He gives in Revelation should strike terror in the hearts of all. Those who are saved now should live godly, soberly and righteously, looking forward to the coming of the Lord in the air. (See Titus 2:11-14.) If they are truly the Lord's they will be with Him in Heaven during the tribulation on earth. But what about those who will be left here on earth because they do not know the Lord? Are your students concerned for them? They should be! May your own concern, teacher, inspire your students to be good witnesses.

A chart showing the meaning of the symbols used in this lesson is found on page 9.

Scripture to be studied: Revelation 8–11

The *aim* of the lesson: To show that these coming judgments will be used of God to break down the dominion of sin over this earth.

What your students should *know*: Although God will send many warnings, the people will not repent.

What your students should *feel*: An urgency for sharing the Gospel with others who will otherwise go through this period of judgments.

What your students should *do*: Pray much for those who do not know Christ and determine how they can warn them of the tribulation.

Lesson outline (for the teacher's and students' notebooks):
1. Six trumpet judgments (Revelation 8:1–9:21).
2. The mighty angel and the little book (Revelation 10:1-11).
3. The two witnesses (Revelation 11:1-14).
4. The seventh trumpet (Revelation 11:15-19).

The verse to be memorized:

Shall not the Judge of all the earth do right?
(Genesis 18:25b)

THE LESSON

Has God ever sent judgments upon the earth? Indeed, He has. Thousands of years ago the people of Israel were held captive in Egypt. God had promised them a land of their own. But the king of Egypt would not let the people go. God sent terrible judgments upon the land of Egypt. The waters were turned to blood. Frogs, lice and flies covered everything. The Egyptians' animals became sick, and the people ached with painful boils. Giant hailstones, fire and locusts destroyed the crops. Darkness covered the land. Finally the oldest son in every Egyptian family was killed. (See Exodus 7–12. If you want illustrations, use Old Testament Volume #7 *Redemption*.)

At last, Pharaoh let the people leave the land. God's judgments were real and severe.

In our lesson today, we will learn of more judgments that are going to come upon the whole earth. (*Teacher:* Using illustrations, review the judgments of Lesson #1.) What does the Bible call this time of judgment? *(The tribulation)* Will those who have believed in Christ *before* the tribulation begins, be on the earth? *(No.)* Where will they be? *(In Heaven)* How will they have gone to Heaven? *(The Lord Jesus will come in the air, and they will be caught up to be with Him in Heaven.)*

Will people turn to Christ during the tribulation? *(Yes.)* Who? *(144,000 Jews; many others from every part of the world)* Will they have peaceful, happy lives during the tribulation? *(No, many will be martyred.)* How will the 144,000 newly saved Jews be protected during the tribulation? *(God will put His mark of ownership on each one.)*

Almost 2,000 years ago the Lord God showed John things which will take place some future day. He saw that when Christ the Lord opened the seventh seal, seven angels appeared. Each was given a trumpet.

Before the angels sounded their trumpets, another angel stood at the golden altar in Heaven. There he offered perfumed incense to God. This incense pictures the prayers of the tribulation believers. (See Revelation 6:1-11.) The smoke of the incense and the prayers of the believers arose to God. And God would answer their prayers.

The angel then filled the golden cup with fire from the altar (of Judgment), and hurled the fire to earth. Immediately there were loud thunderings, bright flashes of lightning and a great earthquake. God was about to send more judgments to earth.

1. SIX TRUMPET JUDGMENTS
Revelation 8:1–9:21

Show Illustration #6A

The first angel blew his trumpet. Hail, fire and blood came down upon the earth. All the grass was burned and a third of the trees burned to the ground. So it will be during the tribulation. (*Teacher:* Add red color to illustration indicating blood on Earth, on the falling "mountain," and the bloody sea.)

The second angel sounded his trumpet. Something huge, burning with fire was thrown into the sea. A third of the sea turned to blood. (Show center of Illustration #6.) A third of the fish died, and a third of the ships were destroyed. Imagine what that will be like during the tribulation!

The trumpet of the third angel sounded. And a large, burning star (named Wormwood) fell from Heaven into the rivers. This poisoned one-third of the rivers. And those who drank the water, died. Will this terrify people during the tribulation?

Angel number four sounded his trumpet. A third of the sun, moon and stars were darkened: a third part of the day and night had no light. Think what that will mean during the tribulation.

Suddenly another angel flew through Heaven, crying loudly, "Woe, woe, woe!" This meant it would be bad, bad, bad for the people on earth when the next three trumpets sounded.

Show Illustration #6B

The fifth angel sounded his trumpet. John saw a star which had previously fallen from Heaven to earth. This star was different from the stars we see in the sky. This star pictures a living being. He was given the key to the bottomless pit (a great hole without a bottom, an abyss). The bottomless pit is a place where some of the demons and evil spirits are locked up. With the key, the living being opened the bottomless pit. And a big cloud of smoke came up from the pit, darkening the sun.

Out of the smoke came strange creatures which spread over the earth. They were ordered not to hurt the grass or plants or trees. They were told to hurt *people* but only those who did not have the seal of God on their foreheads. Who had God's seal? (See Revelation 7:2-8.) For five months these creatures were allowed to attack people and give them much pain. However, they were not permitted to kill anyone. But the pain was so bad that men wanted to die. (*Teacher:* Point to the two figures on the bottom left of Illustration #6.) Some even tried to kill themselves, but they could not do it.

These evil creatures had a king over them. His name is Apollyon, or Satan. (His name means *destroyer.*) He was head over the bottomless pit. God will send this judgment too during the tribulation!

Angel number six sounded his trumpet. John heard a voice commanding, "Let the four angels loose who have been chained at the river (Euphrates)." These evil angels were prepared for the purpose of killing a third of the human race. Then appeared a great army of 200,000,000 soldiers (on horses for swift movement). With fire, smoke and brimstone (weapons of hell), they killed one-third of the people on earth.

When this happens during the coming tribulation, will the people who remain on earth turn to the Lord? No, they will not. Instead they will continue to worship demons (compare 1 Timothy 4:1) and false, make-believe gods (idols).

One trumpet judgment was left. But before the seventh angel blew this trumpet, John saw something else in Heaven.

2. THE MIGHTY ANGEL AND THE LITTLE BOOK
Revelation 10:1-11

Another strong, shining angel came down from Heaven, holding an open scroll in his hand. Like a conqueror, he stood with one foot on the sea and the other on land. Loudly he announced, "There will be no more waiting. When the seventh angel sounds his trumpet, the mystery of God will be finished."

A voice from Heaven commanded John, "Go, take the little open scroll from the hand of the angel who is standing on the sea and land." John obeyed, and the angel continued, "Take it and eat it. It will taste like honey in your mouth. But it will be bitter in your stomach."

John did as he was told. And it *was* sweet. But *after* he swallowed it, it was bitter in his stomach. What did all this mean?

Show Illustration #7A

That little scroll had the revelations from God in it. Those revelations told that the plan of God will be fulfilled and the Lord Jesus *will* rule the earth. This was good news and was like honey to John.

Show Illustration #7B

But the sad, bitter part was that it would take more judgments to bring about God's plan.

3. THE TWO WITNESSES
Revelation 11:1-14

Then John saw two men dressed in rough cloth made from the hair of animals. They were two special witnesses for God.

When these two powerful men are on earth during the tribulation, they will: (1) kill their enemies with fire, (2) have power to keep it from raining; (3) turn the waters to blood; and (4) bring plagues upon the earth.

After three and one half years (some think at the middle of the tribulation; others understand it to be at the end of the tribulation), the beast (or monster) will come out of the bottomless pit. He will fight against the two men and kill them. The people on earth will be so happy about their deaths, they will celebrate as if it were Christmas. They will send gifts to one another. Instead of burying the two men, the people will let them lie on the streets of Jerusalem. For three and one half days people from all over the world will come to gawk at the two dead bodies.

But after three and one half days of merrymaking, the people will be terrified. For God will bring the two men back to life. A loud voice from Heaven will call, "Come up here!"

Show Illustration #8

And the two men will go up to Heaven in a glory cloud. At that moment there will be a great earthquake. One-tenth of the city of Jerusalem will be destroyed and 7,000 people will die. And, believe it or not, those left on earth will give praise to God!

4. THE SEVENTH TRUMPET
Revelation 11:15-19

With the sounding of the seventh trumpet, loud voices made an announcement from Heaven: "The kingdom of the world has become the kingdom of our Lord and of His Christ. And He shall reign forever." Christ will soon rule over the world. (See Isaiah 9:6-7.)

Hearing this, the 24 elders (representing the believers) rose from their thrones. They fell before God and worshiped Him saying, "We thank You, O Lord God Almighty, the eternal One, because You are ruling with Your great power. The people who do not know You, God, are angry with You. But now You are angry with *them*. It is time for the wicked dead to be judged. It is time for You to reward the righteous."

Some future day all of this will happen. It will be glorious for the righteous! But what a terrible time it will be for those who would not believe in the Lord!

Show Illustration #9

John saw 2,000 years ago that the temple of God in Heaven was opened. He could see the ark of the covenant inside the temple. (In God's temple on earth, the ark had been the place of the presence of God.) The ark which shone from the temple in Heaven reminded believers that God is faithful and will be with those who belong to Him–even through the final judgment on earth.

At the end of the seventh trumpet judgment, there were flashes of lightning, loud thunderings, large hailstones and an earthquake.

God gave all these warnings long ago. John wrote them down. From these we know something of the wrath of God. We know that He, the Judge of all the earth, will do what is right. If you do not belong to God through trusting in His Son, you will be punished and separated from Him forever and ever. But God doesn't want to punish you. You can have forgiveness of sin now and assurance of everlasting life by receiving the Lord Jesus as your Saviour.

Are you already a child of God? If so, are you faithfully warning those who are not in the family of God of the judgments to come? Will you list in your notebook the names of those to whom you want to witness this week?

Lesson 3

THE WAR (ON EARTH AND IN HEAVEN)

NOTE TO THE TEACHER

Throughout this lesson you will observe the constant conflict between God and Satan, between good and evil. Satan is a liar and the father of lies. He is deceitful, especially because he often imitates the things of God. God sows good seed. Satan sows weeds and bad seed. But, as Jesus said, they sometimes look so much alike that we are not able to tell them apart. (See Matthew 13:28-30.)

God sent His Son, the Lord Jesus Christ, to this earth as a Man to represent God. Satan will raise up the Beast King, a man of earth, who will represent him in all his evil. God reveals Himself in a Holy Trinity (Father, Son and Holy Spirit). Satan reveals himself in the form of an evil trinity (Satan, the Beast and the False Prophet). During the days of tribulation, man will be given the choice of worshiping Satan and the Beast, or God and His Christ.

Remember, after Christ takes His church (all believers) to be with Himself, there will not be one true Christian left on earth. But God will have a witness here. There will be Bibles, Christian literature and taped radio and TV programs. Some will read and hear and believe in the Lord Jesus Christ. So God will again have witnesses. If you feel you can't teach all of this at one time, then teach it in two lessons. Encourage students to read aloud the Revelation verses in class. They should mark in their Bibles the meanings of the symbols. You, teacher, must study *thoroughly*.

Do you have the books on Revelation which we recommend in Volume #43? If so, you will see that we understand the meanings of the symbols used in this lesson as listed on the chart on page 9.

Scripture to be studied: Revelation 12–14

The *aim* of the lesson: To show that God has the right to be angry with Satan, the great deceiver.

   What your students should *know*: That Satan is a clever imitator and deceiver.

   What your students should *feel*: Aware that Satan can deceive them now; a desire to obey God rather than Satan.

   What your students should *do*: Be watchful so they will not be tricked by Satan.

Lesson outline (for the teacher's and students' notebooks):

1. War in Heaven and on earth (Revelation 12:1-17).
2. The unholy trinity (Revelation 13:1-18).
3. The Lamb and 144,000 (Revelation 14:1-5).
4. Four warnings (Revelation 14:6-20).

The verse to be memorized:

   Shall not the Judge of all the earth do right?
   (Genesis 18:25b)

THE LESSON

Almost 2,000 years ago, the Apostle John had a preview of the future. God showed him things that have not yet happened. But they will take place exactly as God has planned.

Hundreds of years before John's time, there lived a boy named Joseph. Joseph had 11 brothers. (See Genesis 37:5-11.) And he had many dreams. In those days, with no Bible through which God could speak, dreams *sometimes* had very special meanings.

In one of Joseph's dreams, the sun, moon and 11 stars all bowed down before him. The sun represented his father, Jacob; the moon, his mother. The 11 stars stood for Joseph's 11 brothers. The sun, moon and stars were signs of what was going to happen. Years later Joseph became a ruler in Egypt and ruled over his family–who had to bow before him, just as he had dreamed. (See Genesis 37:9-10; 42:1–47:31.) This family had a special place in the plan of God, though they didn't realize how important they were. God planned that a whole nation would come from them–the nation of Israel, made up of 12 tribes.

1. WAR IN HEAVEN AND ON EARTH
Revelation 12:1-17

In Revelation chapter 12 is the record of John's seeing a special sign. He saw a woman dressed with the sun. The moon was under her feet. On her head was a crown with twelve stars. What did it mean? Well, the sun, moon and stars in *Joseph's* dream spoke of Joseph's family which became the nation Israel. The sign which *John* saw also spoke of the nation Israel. The woman represented Israel, the nation with the 12 tribes.

What John saw next was actually a review of things which had already happened on earth. He saw that a baby boy, Christ, the Messiah, was born into the nation of Israel. (See Revelation 12:2, 5a.) But before Christ came to earth, something dreadful had happened in Heaven. A beautiful angel called Lucifer rebelled against God. (See Isaiah 14:12-15.) And he caused one-third of the angels to turn against God, too. (See Jude 6; Revelation 12:4a.)

Show Illustration #10

God threw the beautiful angel out of Heaven. And Lucifer, son of the morning, became Satan. Satan could not rule in Heaven. So he became prince of the power of the air. (See Ephesians 2:2.) The other evil angels became his helpers.

John saw (up in Heaven) a fierce, red dragon which had great power. (See Revelation 12:3.) John knew, of course, that King Herod had tried to kill the baby Jesus as soon as He was born. John knew that the religious leaders of Israel had hated the Lord Jesus–even crucified Him. Now it was perfectly clear that Herod and the Jewish religious leaders had been controlled by the dragon. And that dragon was Satan. (See Revelation 12:9.) He is the one who wanted to destroy the Son of God. He had planned to ruin all of God's program.

But Satan could not win, even when Jesus died on the cross. For God's Son rose from the grave. Then after 40 days, He was taken up to God and His throne in Heaven. (Read Revelation 12:5, end of verse.) Satan, the dragon, could not destroy the Lord Jesus there. What would Satan do now?

The next thing John saw was a war which is going to take place in Heaven during the coming tribulation. (Read Revelation 12:7-12.) Satan, as always, will still be allowed to go up to Heaven to accuse the believers. (See Revelation 12:10; Job 1:6.) His evil angels will be with him. But Michael, one of God's highest angels, and many other good angels of God will fight against Satan and his helpers. What a fight that will be! Good against evil. Evil against good. Who will win? Satan will be fierce and strong as a dragon. But God's good angels will be stronger. And they will win the battle. Then Satan and his evil helpers will be cast down to the earth. Satan will have been defeated once again.

This will make Satan so angry, that he will turn against Israel, the woman who had given birth to Christ. (See Revelation 12:13-17; Matthew 24:15-21.) He will chase the people of Israel and try to hurt them.

The people of Israel will run away into a desert where no people live. This will be a safe place prepared by God. (Remember: 144,000 Israelites will have been saved early in the tribulation.) In the desert place, God will care for His people, Israel, for three and one half years, the last half of the tribulation. (The 1,260 days of Revelation 12:6 equals three and one half years.)

Since the devil will not be able to capture the people of Israel, he will fight against others on earth who are on God's side. (Remember, the 144,000 saved Israelites will witness for the Lord Jesus. People from all over the world will turn to Him.)

2. THE UNHOLY TRINITY
Revelation 13:1-18

Suddenly John saw a powerful beast. (See Revelation 13:1-5.) During the future years of tribulation, the beast which John saw will be the Man of Sin. (See 2 Thessalonians 2:3.) He is against Christ –anti-Christ. There will be ten kings (which is the meaning of the ten horns, Revelation 13:1) who will give their power and authority to this anti-Christ. (See Revelation 17:12-13.) He will be a man of great power. And his power will come from Satan. (See Revelation 13: 2b.)

The people who will be on earth during the coming tribulation will follow this evil man–anti-Christ. For 42 months (three and one half years) he will kill many who have trusted in Christ during the tribulation. (See Revelation 13:7.) The earth dwellers who are *unbelievers* will worship this anti-Christ *and* the one who controls him–Satan. (See Revelation 13:8, 15.)

There will be another evil man at work during the tribulation. (John saw him as a "beast coming out of the earth"–Revelation 13:11.) He will have power to do unbelievable miracles–as the prophets of God did long ago. This man will be a false prophet. He will cause fire to come down from Heaven to earth. (Read Revelation 13:13.) He will make an image of anti-Christ and cause it to come to life! (See Revelation 13:14-15.)

So Satan will try to imitate God the Father, God the Son and God the Holy Spirit with his unholy, evil trinity. The three evil ones are Satan, the Man of Sin (the anti-Christ) and the False Prophet. What a deceiver Satan is! What an imitator!

Show Illustration #11

The false prophet will give a command to place a mark on everyone, on the right hand or the forehead. No one will be allowed to buy or sell anything without this mark. Rich or poor, old or young will have to receive the name of anti-Christ or the number of his name– 666. (*Teacher:* Point to figures on left of illustration.)

3. THE LAMB AND THE 144,000
Revelation 14:1-5

While these awful things will be taking place on earth during the tribulation, John saw something wonderful that will happen.

Show Illustration #12

The 144,000 Israelites who were saved and received the mark of God's ownership, will be with God the Son. Do you remember how God had kept them safe from Satan? (See Revelation 12:14-16.) And they will be singing! These 144,000 will have been brought safely out of the tribulation of earth. They will have kept themselves pure from the evil of the world. And they will have followed the Lamb of God. (See Revelation 14:4.)

4. FOUR WARNINGS
Revelation 14:6-20

Long ago, John saw up in Heaven a preview of something else that will happen in the future time of tribulation.

Show Illustration #13A

An angel will announce the Gospel message to all people on earth. Up to this time, *people* will have done all the preaching of the Gospel. But before the end of the great tribulation, a holy angel of God will warn people, giving them one final chance to be saved.

Show Illustration #13B

Another angel will give a second warning. He will say that the headquarters of Satan's Man of Sin, the sinful city, is about to fall. (See Revelation 14:8. Babylon was a famous city on the Euphrates River. In Revelation it seems to be a symbol of Rome. There will be a false religious system that will center in the city on seven hills, which is Rome. (See Revelation 17:1-9.)

Show Illustration #13C

A third angel will give another warning: "Anyone who worships the Man of Sin, who is anti-Christ, and his statue, and has received his mark, will have the anger of God on him. He will be punished with fire and burning sulphur forever." (See Revelation 14:9-11.)

But what will happen to those who will *not* worship the Beast and will be put to death? (See Revelation 14:12-13.) They will be safe with the Lord forever. And their good works will follow them to Heaven.

A fourth angel will cry out to God the Son, "Begin to use your sickle." (See Revelation 14:14-16.) It will then be judgment time! At last, all people, great and small, will have to stand before the Lord, Creator of all.

If you know Christ as your Saviour and Lord, you don't need to fear the awful time of judgment that is ahead. But are you living today so that you will not be ashamed when you stand before God? Will you have family and friends with you–people you have introduced to the Lord? Don't let Satan trick you into being afraid to witness for Christ. List in your notebook the names of those to whom you want to give the Gospel this week.

Lesson 4
THE SEVEN BOWL JUDGMENTS

NOTE TO THE TEACHER

Rebellion must be put down before Christ sets up His kingdom. God's wise judgment will put an end forever to evil and the enemies of God. Through His judgments He will cleanse the earth and reclaim His rightful ownership. It is a glorious thing to be on God's side!

Our understanding of the symbols used in this lesson are listed in the chart on page 28. (Those explained in the text are not included.) Your students should list these in their notebooks. In their Bibles, at the verses mentioned, they should enter the meanings of the symbols.

Scripture to be studied: Revelation 15–18

The *aim* of the lesson: God rules! Even through the evil which men do, God will bring about His own plan.

  What your students should *know*: That God is great and holy. Sinful men cannot defy God and get away with it.

  What your students should *feel*: A hatred for evil.

  What your students should *do*: Turn away from sinful practices and look for God's Son to come from Heaven for His own.

Lesson outline (for the teacher's and students' notebooks):
1. Preparation for the bowl judgments (Revelation 15:1-8).
2. The seven bowl judgments (Revelation 16:1-21).
3. Attack against the wicked city (Revelation 17).
4. The fall of the wicked city (Revelation 18).

The verse to be memorized:

Shall not the Judge of all the earth do right?
(Genesis 18:25b)

THE LESSON

God hates sin. He has always hated it. He always will hate it. Sin must be punished. And God, the Judge of all the earth, will do right when He punishes sin.

Before time began, God planned a program. Much that He planned in His program has already taken place. The next big event will be the coming of His Son in the air. All who truly have the Lord Jesus as their Saviour will be caught up to meet the Lord in the air. They will then be with the Lord wherever He is. What a glorious day it will be when believers will be caught up to Heaven!

But, oh, how dreadful it will be for those who remain on earth. (*Teacher:* You may wish to use the illustrations of some of the judgments God will send during the coming tribulation.) There will be wars, famine, death. People who will turn to the Lord will be murdered. There will be fire and earthquakes.

Trees and grass will be burned up. Many waters of earth will be turned to blood, and drinking water will be poisoned. Most people will be deceived and worship Satan's man. As a result, they will be tormented with fire and sulphur forever. God hates all sin and will punish it. Even so, the earth dwellers will not turn to Him. So He will send more judgments.

1. PREPARATION FOR THE BOWL JUDGMENTS
Revelation 15:1-8

God showed John what the rest of the judgments will be. Before John saw them, God revealed that there will be many happy people in Heaven. There nothing will be able to hurt them.

Show Illustration #14

They will have been put to death on earth for having turned to the Lord during the tribulation (Revelation 15:2-4). But in Heaven they will have harps and sing this praise to God: "O Lord God, the Almighty; righteous and true are Your ways. . . ." They had been murdered. But they will understand that all of God's ways are right.

Then seven angels will be given golden bowls. These bowls will be filled with the anger of God. And a voice will command, "Go and pour out the bowls of the anger of God upon the earth." (See Revelation 15:5-8.)

2. THE SEVEN BOWL JUDGMENTS
Revelation 16:1-21

Show Illustration #15

(*Teacher:* As each judgment is mentioned, point to the appropriate number.)

The first angel will pour out bowl #1. (Read Revelation 16:1-2.) This judgment will bring terrible and painful sores upon the people who will have the mark of Satan's man–the Man of Sin (# 666). They are the ones who will have worshiped his image. Only those who will love and believe God will escape the horrible sores. For God will protect them.

The second angel will pour out his bowl of judgment. (Read Revelation 16:3.) The water in the sea will turn to blood. And every living thing in the sea will die. (Previously, in the second trumpet judgment, a third of the sea was turned to blood.)

The third angel will pour out his bowl upon the rivers and they will turn to blood. (Read Revelation 16:4, 7.) Then the wicked people of earth will have only blood to drink. This will be the punishment they deserve for murdering people who turned to the Lord during the tribulation.

The fourth angel will pour out his bowl on the sun. (Read Revelation 16:8-9.) And the sun will be given power to burn with its heat. As people on earth are burned by this, and they will use bad language about God. But they will not be sorry for their sins. Nor will they turn to God.

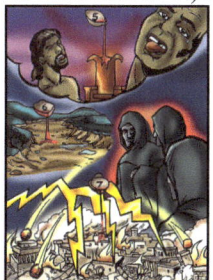

Show Illustration #16

(As in Illustration #15, point to the numbered judgments in order.)

The fifth angel will pour out his bowl of God's anger upon the throne of the Man of Sin. He is the man who will be against God (that is, the anti-Christ) during the tribulation. (Read Revelation 16:10-11.) His kingdom will become darkened and the people will gnaw their tongues because of pain. But they will not be sorry for their evil and turn to God. Indeed, they will use bad language about God.

Then the sixth angel will pour out his bowl on the great Euphrates River and it will be dried up. (See Revelation 16:12.) This river is east of Jerusalem and over 1,700 miles long. God is going to make a way for armies from the East to get to the place where the last great battle on earth will be fought. (We will learn more about this later.)

Before the seventh judgment bowl, three demons (Revelation 16:14) will come from the unholy trinity. (Do you remember them? Satan, the Man of Sin and the False Prophet. Point to the center right of Illustration #16; then read Revelation 16:13-16.)

In an amazing way, they will go to the kings of the whole world and cause them all to come together to a place north of Jerusalem called Armageddon. (Armageddon, or Meggido, is in the Plain of Esdraelon.) They will come to this place to fight against God Almighty. (We will learn more about this battle later on.) But these evil ones will not realize that God is allowing them to bring about what He had planned from the very beginning of time!

Meanwhile, people on earth will again be warned to be pure and watchful (Revelation 16:15). God still yearns for people who have rejected His Son to turn to Him. He knows how horrible the future will be for those who refuse His love.

The seventh angel will pour out the last judgment. An announcement will be made, "It is done!"

There will be thunder, lightning and the most dreadful earthquake of all time. (Read Revelation 16:17-21.) Great cities will crumble, islands and mountains will disappear. Huge hailstones will fall upon people. But instead of their turning to God for forgiveness, they will again use bad language about Him.

3. ATTACK AGAINST THE WICKED CITY
Revelation 17

John needed an explanation of what God next showed him about the future. (*Teacher:* Read Revelation 17:1-7. For the meaning, read 17:8-18.)

We have learned that after the rapture of Christian believers, the tribulation will begin on earth. When it begins, there will be much religion on earth. But the many people (Revelation 17:15) who seem to be religious will not be faithful to the Lord. They will be like a woman (a harlot) who is not faithful to her husband.

This group with the false religion will have great wealth. It will reign gloriously during the first half of the tribulation. (See Revelation 17:4.) This false religious group is named Babylon (see Revelation 17:5). The name is called "a mystery" which means it is a secret use of the word. The meaning of the mystery name is Rome, a city of seven hills. (Read Revelation 17:9-18.) Many groups, all pretending to worship God, will belong to this one huge false church. But they will not trust in Jesus Christ, God the Son. The people in this church will murder those who will be turning to the Lord Jesus Christ during the tribulation. (Read Revelation 17:6.)

Show Illustration #17

After a while, ten kings (Revelation 17:12) will join with the Man of Sin and destroy Rome (point to top of illustration), the headquarters of the false church. (See Revelation 17:16.) Evil will fight against evil for it will be God's way of working out His program. (See Revelation 17:17.)

4. THE FALL OF THE WICKED CITY
Revelation 18

Not only will the religious part of the city be destroyed but the business part will also lie in ruins. It will become the living place of demons and every kind of unclean spirit. Dirty, hated birds will be there. (Read Revelation 18:2.) God will remember all of the sinfulness. He, the Judge of all the earth, will do right by sending speedy judgment to that wicked place. (Read Revelation 18:8.)

In one day everything will be gone. There will be no more gold, silver, jewels, fine cloth, expensive wood, no more ivory  or marble. The sweet-smelling spices and perfumes will be destroyed. All the wine, oil, flour, wheat, cattle, sheep and horses will be gone.

Show Illustration #18A

The shipmasters, sailors, traders, the buyers and the sellers will put dust on their heads and weep. They will cry, but not for their sins, nor for the sins of Rome. But they will weep because they will not be able to make lots of money as they had in the past. (See Revelation 18:17-19.)

Show Illustration 18B

The people on earth will be crying. But in Heaven there will be great rejoicing. (*Teacher:* Read Revelation 18:20.) Why? Because God will have answered the prayers of His people. He will judge the evildoers–those who killed His children. God will do what is just and right. For He, the Judge of all the earth, always does right.

Now *you* have been warned of the judgments that God will send to earth during the tribulation. They will be fierce and terrible. But you will not experience them if you are a child of God. Only those who refuse to receive Him will remain on the earth after believers are raptured–caught up to Heaven with the Lord. Let me ask you: are you truly in the family of God through trusting in the Lord Jesus Christ? If not, will you turn to Him right now? If you will, please tell me after class so I can help you.

If you are already God's own, with whom will you share the Good News of salvation this week? Write the names of these people in your notebook. Then we shall ask the Lord to make you a bold witness for Him.

SEAL	PASSAGE	SYMBOL	MEANING
#1	Rev. 6:2	White horse, rider with crown and bow	This is a deceiver who is against Christ. He will talk of peace but have war in his heart.
#2	Rev. 6:4	Red horse, rider with sword	A warning of bloodshed in war
#3	Rev. 6:5-6	Black horse, rider with scales	A warning of famine
#4	Rev. 6:8	Sickly, yellowish green horse, rider named "Death"	A warning of death
#5	Rev. 6:9-11	Souls under the altar in Heaven	People martyred for testifying of Christ, calling for revenge
#6	Rev. 6:12-17	Earthquake, sun, moon, stars and skies affected	God will upset certain things in the universe He created.
#7	Rev. 7:1-3	Angel with the seal of God	A superior angel will mark the 144,000 Jews who turn to Christ during the tribulation. Because of the mark, they will be kept safe from their enemies.

PASSAGE	SYMBOL	MEANING
Rev. 9:1	A star which fell to the earth	Satan, who fell from Heaven to the earth (See Isaiah 14:12-15; Luke 10:18.)
Rev. 9:2	The bottomless pit	The abode of demons (See Luke 8:31.)
Rev. 9:3-10	Locusts	Demons who take the form of locusts (See Revelation 9:11.)
Rev. 9:11	King of the locusts	Satan, or Apollyon, the destroyer

PASSAGE	SYMBOL	MEANING
Rev. 12:1	The woman with a crown of 12 stars	The nation of Israel
Rev. 12:3-4	The dragon	Satan
Rev. 12:4	A third of the stars of Heaven	The angels who rebelled with Satan and were thrown out of Heaven
Rev. 12:5	A Child caught up to God	The ascension of the Lord Jesus
Rev. 13:1	A beast out of the sea, with ten horns and seven heads	This is the Man of Sin who is against Christ (the anti-Christ)
Rev. 13:2	The dragon who gives power to the beast	Satan gives his power to the anti-Christ
Rev. 13:11	Another beast	A false prophet who will force people to worship the anti-Christ
Rev. 13:18	666	A mark which will identify those who follow the anti-Christ
Rev. 14:1	The Lamb	The Lord Jesus Christ
Rev. 14:8	Babylon	Rome, the city on seven hills

PASSAGE	SYMBOL	MEANING
Rev. 16:12	The kings of the East	The armies of the nations of the Orient
Rev. 16:13	The dragon	Satan
Rev. 16:13	The beast	The Man of Sin who is against Christ (the anti-Christ)
Rev. 16:19	The great city	This may refer to Jerusalem. (See Rev. 11:18; compare to Zechariah 14:4.)
Rev. 17:12	Ten kings	Ten nations will unite in the West and be headed by the anti-Christ (See Daniel 7:23-24.)
Rev. 17:12	One hour	For one purpose
Rev. 17:15	Peoples, multitudes, nations, tongues	The false church will be worldwide

www.ingramcontent.com/pod-product-compliance
Lightning Source LLC
Chambersburg PA
CBHW060801090426
42736CB00002B/118